Mystic Knowing

Mystic Knowing

Jeremy Garcia

Pep Talk

Tender bliss,
     Comes from knowing today I did not sin,
Wonder Swiss,
Gets confirm by praying to Creator on the regular,
Make belief,
Is strong for Creator depends on you to believe,
Shake relief,
Obey the law and achieve mystic life,

Being Discharged

Be away from wrong,
    Political correct,
Yet impacts guide the darkness,
Alive still to achieve prosperity,
Tell yourself to be strong,
Godly dialect,
Yet reality shows the darkness,
Alive in will to seek prosperity,
How I made it this long?
Consequence effect,
Yet I know I am out of the darkness,
Alive for bested to obey father in his prosperity,

What Would Jesus Do!

My neighbor smokes crack,
   Stable to keep it going,
With tunnel vision of sin is regularly,
Smooth cool man appearance,
Forgive the sin and pray behind the back,
Stable to keep it flowing,
With tunnel vision for sin residue clearly,
Smooth tool stand clearance,
The faith of love for neighbor to see light is by praying through Jesus to Creator on sight,

Informed

Aware of Creator,
　　Believing built consciousness,
Pin pointed to be clear from sinning,
Beware of Creator,
Believing in obedience opens a everlasting world,
Pin pointed to not be with the blind in sinning,
Sight of Creator,
Determined in Jesus's path,
Believing comes reward in being of godly,
Pin pointed to be of no wickedness,
Light of Creator,
Detailed in Jesus's wrath,
Believing in obedience keeps you loved eternally,
Pin pointed to know life without wickedness,

Acknowledgement of Her

Guide me to paradise,
      Let me see the soul of the king through your eyes,
Strangers in harmony among the crowd,
Sin dying in our arms of holiness proud,
Getting rewarded of promises from Creator as ascended in the skies,
Being in sync of obedience as the darken angels' fries,
Guide me to paradise,
Shine the glory of peace from your eyes,
Sight me to caressing blissful mindset,
Forgive and become of godly from what lies met,
Become tender to forgive the darkness skies,
Be in wonderful protection as a stinger flies,
Guide me to everlasting paradise
From your existence intertwine in thoughts of loving me with your honest eyes,

Dead Single Dad, Alive Single Son

The know of him gets me closer to God,
    The known of him has sin close to the heart of living,
The king comes between us in delight direction,
Both waiting for a queen to shine perfection of living life,
He mate and birth me,
I mate and unborn glee,
The path has a lady in will of romance after all is done,
After I go unconscious to her with him giving me trust in
Creator for it's been done,
    I be back in wake in his and mine desire for the queen,

Came a Hollar

Suddenly it happen again,
Death surrounds the picture of best in living without sin,
Memories strengthens in loving the deceased still,
Apart of me forever in faith as the kingdom doors opens at will,
I carry the dead on with me to the maker,
I very be dead too yet Jesus Christ is reality to me in obedience as he comes back to earth to awake her,
I live the continuance of the dead for hope,
I give in continuance with the dead by hope,
In meeting them in the kingdom of the father,
Suddenly death a'came holler,

Only In This Life They Live Among You

The darkness of them not having relations with the father,
Simple smiles Neva existed in them,
No change for the better in the moments that matter,
Like rivers without the otter,
No detail help of the current of the life of the water with them,
They drown while the water gets fatter,
I swim with ease in receiving love and peace from relations with the father,

That Married One

He dances in faith,
She godly speaks,
Come to know forgiveness,
They both prove in ceremony,
She dies first,
He dances his last faithful breath,
Their energy activates the Holy Spirit,
Being loved while in love to have intelligence of the Creator to inherent,

Destiny

Immoral thoughts holding a toy gun,
    Sanity shines along the way as if seeing a dandelion between the sidewalk,
    It's hope from a nation under God and mostly his care,
    To acknowledge the sight of righteous in cherished obedience for morality,
    Yet its nature one would break the dandelion by parting it from its roots to hold and eventually toss away,

Friendly Gesture

Walking, seeing houses,
    Heart feels faith for neighbors,
A nature as a cat skillful to catch mousses,
With the little rodent taste it savors,
To be directed away from sin and see the choice,
As I best be obedient to Creator with my chosen decision,
I pray for a miracle in my alone time in godliness rejoice,
So I walk in hope to make a tender collision,

Self Revelation

L ost in sin,
    Host with grin,
Shackles tight,
Wacky might,
Was the cause of the downfall,
How I hurt and the path of life begins to befall,
Into a invisible relationship to the visible words of the king,
In believing with trusting the concept of Jesus Christ as I hear nature sing,
The reality of the return of him in what he said,
It came to me in imprisonment the close home of torment and the garnishing of teeth among concrete bed,

Told It Was Natural

Didn't know it was human nature till it happen,
Years in front of me said we are naturally capable,
The chicken doesn't fly yet it wings are flappin,
Without sin this life won't be shape'able,
Now it's human nature only to Christ I belong,
End the wrong tunnel vision and the negative habits,
Struggle for easy love keeps being that strong,
Still I obey being the few white rabbits,
Knowing what I didn't is the awe of living,
Human nature describe by a king and only by this king you are set free,
Capable to understand righteous as the evil giving,
Reality the able to be,
Natural act is shocking when it's a standard, as a women knowing dressing sexy, a man can stand hard,

The Love One Chose Hell

The world is uneven when a love one has gone dead,
Without God its like that one left me,
Holy brew is remembering what the one said,
With God the one with me will always be,
To be not choosing everlasting with the love made,
Without God is the one direction from the get-go,
I know my loved one's truth for our conversation about life will never fade,
With God is I and it happens to be faith to not let go,
Said it will be a distant memory,
Without God is the sea of the next age,
I know now I am Forgiven and forgive the harm of me,
Still the world will always be uneven, only the love of the king can go back to the page,

How I know

As the baby bird lands for the first flight and becomes the might hunter of the sky,

Is me glowing in forgiveness the heading of the king is the ability to get on by,

Still strange power can determine God or no,

Prayer is the ability of the sheep to let the lovely life between Creator and creation know,

The blessing is knowing right from wrong, the answer comes within faith in believing,

Once relations be as obeying the Creator the bad news won't be a hard stress receiving,

All this from believing the word without man, metaphor the scripture in meaning of a Creator and a king is and to be in we the chosen children of the God that never dies,

Faith

The feeling is an awe,
    Not based on what you saw,
Yet giving in by believing,
Once you start the dark begins relieving,
The truth unfolds by this feeling,
Like relief a abstract healing,
The ability of faith keeps the connection to the supreme safe,

What I know

Darken alleys having no connection to the light house,
Them are a sensation in division,
They see out as a flamboyant blouse,
To the king giving one decision,
Yet sin captures your death,
Price paid, still waiting to hear your breath,
The choice of everlasting in dying faith,
Came from hearing your deathly news,
Firm to obey no negativity saithe,
Is the one choice I made seeing the lighthouse,
As I know sinners are sneaky as a mouse,

Imprinted

Decision, make the right one,
    Fall, so natural to sin and be done,
Ability, to know of Creator and obey,
Choice, freewill naturally owning the day,
No knowledge of life's truth is a freebie,

Week To Week

I have no doubts or sorrows on this road of life,
My spirit will still shout and live for tomorrows with no wife,
Because I'm decently calm and collectively confirmed in peace when I pray week to week,
Invisible connection so depth, appearing in trustfully belief,
Reality of gifts in notice giving a such divine relief,
For I'm decently calm and collectively confirmed in peace when I pray week to week,

Sensual Freedom

Shadows of the past,
Entertains with knowing now with a blast,
Gallows had the king,
Intertwine the choice to obey as the heavens and nature sing,
Graves are the beginning of father's heartache,
Realizing obedience in higher knowing to gain more what the heart can take,
While flashbacks, are saddlebacks,
Sin lurks, denied perks,
The shadows form from everlasting,
As the king forgives in multitasking,
I'm free,
I'm in glee,
From the past that shadows my present, with belief in the king with his love be spent,

One Of Today's Thoughts

Faith cleans the house,
Habit of sin is sneaky as a mouse,
The dreams of the blind shapes my bride's blouse,
The shine of freewill leads me to father as a spouse,
The cat eats the mouse,
The habit of sin has no life in this house,
Of the dreams of the blind caresses my bride by a blouse,
Of freewill with father has me wait patiently for a spouse,
My bride gloats the flamboyant blouse,
The care for neighbors to not lose oneself life is the current glow of the house,
The cat as the father waits for another mouse,
To be away from sin with stabilize in righteous is the path in,

To Let You Know

I should've quit you,
    Since the first time, the nice feedback,
  The agreement made long ago,
  To have a voice in the garden while the angels' keep track,
  Lord, knows I be lost without you,
  Since the last time, the romance stills,
  The agreement upholds,
  Wandering in positively of reality in religion feels,
  Should of quit, yet the existence of God's essence comes
from you,
    At the present time, wealth is knowing,
    The agreement everlasting,
    Stable in love as writing of Godly will always be glowing,
    Should've quit you, but the lord shapes innocently among
the darken blue,

Defined Blessing

The chance of blessing,
    Obeying law of the king,
While the blind powerfully guessing,
The children equip in strength of belief of reality in the king,
The blessing basking,
Obeying father among the darkness,
While the blind get no answers to the questions they are asking,
Keeping the belief of God in the darkness,
The blessing's reality,
Obeying the Holy Spirit, to have prayers heard,
Understanding why sin in the world and it's fatality,
The majestic notice of the God will always be heard,
Blessing the act of the Creator in movements, as the show of relations with the Creator in improvement,

A Direction

After the sinful act,
    Light directed to mature,
Realization obeying makes fact,
The dark need no depth,
To consciously be polite in reality's compact,
The shone of the light burns out the flame,
With people of the government jungle making the impact,
After the sinful act I came to know sinner,
My faith not to be the dark in God seals the contract,

Smarten Up

Behind close doors he don't have peace,
Mother sees healthy child,
Daddy murdered, number to early decease,
Devil speaks to his mind, slight wild,
Jesus steps in and forgives become the king,
Still tunnel vision to sin elites,
Vision of religion in the high set to sing,
Alone in the dark he consciously chooses to listen to the steps of the king's feet's,
It was the notice of no worth in the sin of the jungle to behold, and the igniting thrill of truth to unfold,

What It Comes Down To

It was then we live in a savage world,
   Only self can choose live right in it's swirl,
The king can only say the way,
Damn self has to choose that day,
The easy way has no worth,
Self has to ask Father with make believe girth,
Yes the one that paved the savage world to be by oneself choice,
   Ask he to be rejoice,
In steadfast against sin,
Peace then dwells within,
Yet it's hard in this savage world,
Because it's the act to do in its swirl,

That Divine Night

In the mighty earth the king speaks tonight,

Attention is dear, the new age is near, to do wrong I fear, to not be in the passenger seat as the king has steer,

In the mighty earth the king speaks tonight,

Hardship gone in a blink, the something new makes a wink, the glimpse of the next makes you think, weather the boat you on will not sink,

In the mighty earth the king speaks tonight,

Sinners still sin, be of faith to begin, the children of God is no mass its thin, yet the words of he is of wine and gin,

In the mighty earth the king speaks tonite,

Nature and earth become his word, recognize, being the blind is no surprise, thanks to the blessings arise, mental alertness to the ears and eyes,

In the mighty earth the king speaks tonite,

A Enlightenment Of A Neighbor

Druggie is blind,
      Living to the flesh,
I pray for betterment grind,
Giving to spiritually,
Consciousness of knowing right becomes stronger bind,
The will to change for the better is easier to find,
Yet druggie is blind,
I pray for betterment grind,
The light is the reason,
Flesh to spiritually,
End and learn habit is the pleasin,
Awaken to a brighter reality,
The druggie unfold to give up the groove in the betterment mold,

Prison With Conscious

Shackles of sin,
How we to begin?
Shackles of sin,
How all are called and only few are chosen within?
Shackles of sin,
Time made me see the answer, let's begin,

Darken Light

Wicked is the shine,
        Yet truth arise in its find,
The word of father isn't within but behind,
So full of wealth yet don't reach to nine,
Unheard for the choice of don't want,
Absurd is reality righteousness has it taunt,
Wicked doing right, but life has naught,
Lifeless aiming for self sought,
The bride is so loud in the night,
The wicked wise enough to get by in sight,
For mistaken heart in self preference making own light,
Yet it gets darker without a path to get away from the bride's love in might,

Fatherland In The World

Meet me within,
Promise is the natural you are,
In the wild keep me away from sin,
Teach me into betterment that we are,
Meet me within,
Connection is the promise that is,
From being wild, shape me away from sin,
Teach I in betterment , for what lies ahead is,
Kindly meet me there,
The touch of us can please the father,
Master to servant in abundantly care,
Forgiveness in peace without bother,
Kindly meet me there,
Living alive relations to be supreme,
Obedience paying the fare,
Your will in me will be a such beam,
Meet me within, meet me there, kept promises then, in a
life so rare,

Crime

Danced with the devil,
	Never ashamed, yet sorrowful in the Holy Spirit,
Dancing with the devil,
Blasphemy dawned from the war within,
To be damned, not damnful,
To be wiseful , not smarty wise,
Light my fire and see what Godly desire,
Shape my tongue and see what wicked longed,
Dance with the devil,
The enemy no matter what in any level,
Yet all who do are unaware,
But they say they do and make it fair,
Still they naught of a life until clarity,
I'm damned still trying to get a lady to marry me,

Peaceful Thinking

Gentle breeze from the earth spinning delights the mood for the Holy Spirit to give peace,

Struggles end by a blessing, the hurt still hanging on to the word waiting senseless guessing, yet faithful in believing,

Knowledge gain by a blessing, the unaware still reading the word waiting senseless guessing, yet the are calm and be relieving,

Gentle breeze from the earth spinning enlightens the mood for the Holy Spirit to live peace,

The one choice takes time to be made, yet unaware it begins to fade and its made, until the knock-knock happens to be, into your reality see, the choice is to agree as it happens to be,

Gentle breeze from the earth spinning lightens the mood for the Holy Spirit to be peace,

Going Thru the Parley Gates
From The Back Door

Well I'm a back door man!
The mass don't know!
Preachers understand!
Creepin with people trying to live proper with the sinful thinking behind the curtain,
Sleepin on people frying for Jesus Christ in proper armor against sin uncurtain,
I'm a back door man!
The mass don't know!
Preachers understand!
I can talk to my dead dad through the walk of Jesus, would the world believe this? Be in romance with the king until they seize us, still my heart will beat for the king to ease us,
I'm a back door man!
The mass don't know!
Preachers understand!
You better know of peace, where it comes from, know a few will defend its reality, for mystical growth suppress life

with disease, know of from the King's reality in adore mystical growth,

I'm a back door man!

The mass don't know!

Preachers understand!

I know the dead can rise, I pray daily while in fleshy paradise, word of God my wifey eyes, heard her nod, forgiven lies, simplicity in calmness with no surprise, obeying his law living his prize,

I'm a back door man!

The mass don't know!

Preachers understand!

True To Her

She was a wicked doer,
     I saw what God saw,
Sweet innocence life,
After her been a few,
I do what God do,
Sweetheart patience of life,
It only took her to feel love,
I am of God in do,
Bittersweet forgiveness and love life,
She was a heavenly girl,
Being away from God to experience love,
Tender sweet closeness in life,
That one has made impact fully,
From my heart to introduce the father silently from above,
Sweetness precious experience of life,

Pep Talk #2

Listen!
  Yet I just hear,
The devil still couldn't smile,
Bread is Jesus, drink is bloody Christ,
Head believed this, think wits hoody nice,
Still I just did not listen,
Mad depression, sinister to life,
Still the king remain patiently glisten,
Glad succession, win mister in life,
Paradise message in this life,
Is the later age to be more of life,
Listen!
Somehow now I do!

Headline of the Age

Surly I ask forgiveness,
Yet it was my own identity code to mean it,
Obedience, now I have willingness
Yet there is the king when notable fall short,
Surly I ask forgiveness,
Aware it's the season of his return,
Consciousness aims in godly goodness,
Love I self to publish the king's word in I self,
Surly I ask forgiveness,

After Sin

Down the road there is a church,
Yet I am the church,
But the know should be in the head bullets,
It ain't me, I'm no preacher yet I walk with the fortune one,
Fell down at the crossroad to be in betterment,
Still feel forgiveness done,
In the weather spent,
Down the road there is a church,
Yet I know I am the church,

Truth to Neighbor Stacy

Her name echoes through the years,
Bloody red sin,
Yet I'm not the victim as her,
But did not do the act that end her,
Bloody Christ again,
Yet I was a monster like her killer,
But I came to anew in the thriller,
Bloody red sin,
She was a lost little girl,
The one The Doors sung about,
Her bio is a swirl,
A thought to pray about,
Bloody life again,

King Jesus Christ

I desire what the king gives me,
    Peace, calm, nonviolence,
No scheme to hurt, no dream of dirt,
I hire what the king makes me,
Loving parent, loyal friend, enemy to love in silence,
No scheme to hurt, no dream of dirt,
I fire what the king let's me,
Blasphemy, the choice not to follow, sinister til the end no resilience,
No scheme to flirt, no steam to make a quart,
I sire what the king brings me,
The sorrowful, the blind, the sinner in violence,
No scheme to flirt, no steam to make a quart,
I believe I can walk with the king, it's relieve what the talk of the king,

Founding Fathers

Out in the concrete jungle,
Got a hit of a free joint while carrying a bungle,
It's so heavy yet now I can carry it with ease,
The load of what to do in life?
Well a stranger can be a friend,
A friend is family in the times of the return,
Then it click, stay with the gift I've given you said the master,
The gift is the American dream,

The King and I

I see it play at times,
   The attack of the devil,
For I dance with Jesus,
By it from an accident or a sinner with no care,
I faith with godly chimes,
To be protected from the fallen,
For I believe in Jesus,
By it from him the father can bless in care,
I pray for choice away from crimes,
To be wise in the kingdom of the rebuked,
For the lord gives Jesus,
By it from he the world know of peace to care,
I faith no sin in my dimes,
To be clean not wicked filth,
For savior is Jesus,
By the know of he self come to care,

Freedom

Don't know why I had to try to see,
The darken world that permits savagery wickedness,
And I want to take it with me in the heartland of the summer,
Chant the path of sin, drum and dance till father stomps,
Yet free will is the answer,
The choice left to us to do,
Only us to do the righteous,
Behold the son said just pray in my name,
Life been in peace ever since, doubters are bittersweet forgiveness love,
The darken world as well permits light which is good to destroy the savagery wickedness,
Answer is pray for the sinner, and guide myself to do the choice that is godly attended,

God, Earth, and Humanity

He makes me see the world,
    She shelters me in his world,
They are the world,
He is my maker,
She is my home,
They are life,
He makes me live in the world,
She uncovers her breast in his world,
They always the world,
He is the lover,
She only a friend,
They are familiar,
He loves the world,
She mates with us in his world,
They cannot be anything else but the world,
He is the father,
She is the mother,
They are spouse and neighbor,
He is the right side of the world,

She is made of good in his world,
They are the know of the world,

Slight Desire For Love

Before I mate with her again,
　　I had to work on me, being away from sin,
As not to give in the spoils and unstable health,
Only deep thought of the king's word had began,
Hey, I know it's possible to sin,
As not giving in to not care, and ignore proper wealth,
Clarity of what the king needs out of me,
Patience in peace by bested obedience of being free,
Then it shall be in his mood to have me mate with her again,
To know I'm ready for his word to be begun as it began,

Current State

People lost in sin,
     Choosing unwise anger,
  It's influence as liquor gin,
  I'm bless to be in betterment,
  Like a change, yet habits groove and thinking of unjust stops,
  But it's a struggle, Keeping the faithful belief in the king for improvement,
  Persons are victim to sin,
  Innocently trusting the world,
  Not knowing the line to cross isn't thick it's so thin,
  I confess to he to be in relations,
  Peace and calm receive to live on life,
  The ability to properly hate sin and feel it emotionally is one of the best to know revelations,

Troubles

I attend to pray,
    What a relief in knowing,
All alone only the supreme know what I say,
What a belief in growing,
Real meaning to be positive,
Peace comes then it's easy to see the negative,
I attend to pray,
To be in calm away from danger,
Only the innocent know this day,
To know of truth and it couldn't be a stranger,
Real confirms in simple positive,
Ability to notice and consciously not choose the negative,
I attend to pray,

Comes The Decision

The choice to do,
    I accept who I am,
Yet reality is blue
But it was his face surly am,
Knowing the right choice to be,
The rules to follow and agree,
The choice opens a mindset,
Deep wicked thoughts forcefully change into peace,
Consciously knowing life for the first time set,
Being calm through the storms knowing death at ease,
In choosing the right choice to be,
Following the rules into light I agree,

The Choice

No fear or doubt,
    Yet the fallen tries about,
Forgive human and be amount,
On the path with the king, the righteous route,
The wrong fades, as the right shines,
Accept my done, repent as the dark whines,
By obeying in truth I pay my fines,
To unclose the light connection lines,
No tear in darkness,
Yet the enemy only beholds no goodness,
But human made to be good in Creator likeness,
Free will decision the ultimate righteousness,

The Light Of The World

I was lost,
     Heated devil no frost,
It the light in the world that found me,
Clarity of no sin to be,
Picture rise in reality,
The sorrow of my sins isn't my fatality,
Smoking Mary Jane, enlighten the king's pain,
It's the blind, the lost in the lane, precious life gone insane,
Only the king stands in that rain, behold the everlasting grain,
     I was lost,
So wicked not knowing the cost,
It is the light of the world that bound me,
Merry me the king said to be,
Vison is reality,
The tomorrow from my sins isn't my fatality,

The Harden Breeze

Walking feeling the breeze with tension to forgive enemy,
Make the know if I don't forgive it's the end of me,
Light the hardest fire,
It's forgiveness for hire,
You know it's true, it's more darkness if I don't,
Yet it's common sense not to be immaturely won't,
Father enlighten my heart,
Without love what the world will be from the start?
Walking feeling the need with tension from enemy,
Shake the earth father, the rebuked has no end of me,
I will always do the best,
King's law is the reality to all rest,
Journeying in knowing what the tale is to be, hardest point
is no Creator to set me free,

Realizing

The paradise in he is we,
    The honest eyes of he is life in the tree,
I'm bound to obey he while living among we,
I'm ground to say a sinner can be of light in the tree,
Honest truth we don't know until we believe,
In simplest forms the father does relieve,
Once they did bash the ones that do believe,
As the way survives today, it's a relieve,
The world is going to be he,
Harden doubt it will be, but believers will be in refuge to be,
    As life of this will end and only the life alive is in the tree,
It's a relieve, that lively something is always we,

Can't Feel Down

Walk up to me,
Talk of you,
Friendly desire,
Out of the blue,
It's going to take a little bit of me,
The Light between us is only you,
Friend for hire,
Into the darken blue,
Insane once my habit,
Relations in the light,
Friend is the owner of the white rabbit,
By walk up to me with might,

Promise

Please lover don't be slow,
    Cuz I won't be coming home,
The king has his blood thirst in me,
Adapting to be a pong in resistance,
Please lover know you can't be slow,
Cuz the ultimate light is the home,
The king has his bread rehearse in me,
Outcasting the wanting dance as he is my resistance,
Please, lover show you ain't slow,
Forever I await in the kingdom home,
The king is the feast between us to have me,
Living in the truth with resistance,

First Summer Without One

Before the one died, the one said I want to die,
Choices lead to death have been made from the one,
Pick one and be welcome to the things done,
Courage to have lived, Brave enough to cry,
The heat matches the light that was shine in the one,
Remembrance of no harm and polite about the darken natural world,
Experienced love under the darkness in the symbol of light as the sun,
Yet the one direction was wanting to die, the miracle of father in a hurl,
At peace with the mistakes made, awaiting for the next age secured in hope the one has not fade,
I teared for the life had to live by the one, such experience cant be healed by having a Hun,
The healing is death to shed no painful stressful sigh of breath,

Is the sense of the life of the one with realizing the goodness in this stage of the world isn't great as the goodness of father blessing one,

The Trinity In The Wild

Homeless in the concrete jungle searching for the creator,
Light shines from the holy spirit by the king, the door to the creator,
Along this darken yet enlightenment road to know gift,
To know some sort of sign from creator my will swift,
The will to live and accept death from a life with a gift,
Knowing without a home, memories will be a positive drive with a swift,
Homeless in the concrete jungle realizing my gift from the creator,
Light shines from the gift in the holy spirit by the king, the door to the creator,
Along this darken yet enlighten world the know of life is savagely swell,
Some know of the tale, some know by the sound of the bell,
All and most mean all is well,
Yet and but sin is an easy habit to tell,
At home in the concrete jungle being close to the creator,

Best in obedience in the holy spirit by the king, the door to the creator,

The Chance

He conquered them,
	He conquered me,
Them for me,
Me for him,
Bless to see,
Mess to glee,
Shaping me into a child,
From wickedness wild,
Group of law of man the life of footstool,
Being slightly of The king without duel,
The chance to be,
Obedience consumes from free,
Acknowledging I'm a child,
Into the godly wild,
Knowing man law can be a footstool,
From the lively King with fuel,
He conquered them,
He conquered me,
Them for me,

Me for him,

Jesus And The Church

She has intelligence to live this life,
    The key not to sin is living without strife,
She the wife lives up to this,
    As he the husband holds the key with bliss,

Realize

Can't deny the torment,
Can't deny the peace,
Repent is the doormat,
Not to do Immoral from damned knees,
Yet it's the toughest act to do,
The fear of hell ain't it,
It's the knowing it's wrong and you have to take care of who?
The gear to hell aint it,
Hardest is being in the situation,
Consciously the word needs penetration,
Can't deny sin,
Can't deny righteous,
Repent is within,
Only thyself can sight this,
It's so blurred only clarity can see,
It's when Knowingly human meant to be good upon the tough lovely plea,

I nvisibility of the supreme touching my consciousness,
    Realizing goodness from feeling relieved,
Thoughts linger to new horizon consciously,
Proper prayers success life in he I believed,

Divine Sign

Awoke knowing good and evil,
This morning the doorman speaks of judgement,
Quickly I accept what I have done and bless to have time to repent and work on my judgment to not be lethal,
As a toddler seeing fire, reaches towards it suddenly the parent stops the toddler by a shove, I'm happy to know what that nudge meant,

The Current

Worst yet not worsen,
Choice to be cursed among the chosen,
How I faith for neighbors be at peace in stabilized to live their life with their calling of the father,
How I let it bother,
How I see some innocence with power to have peace Hollar,
Still evil exists within and the surrounding,
The serpent confuses the freedom in the founding,
Yet still free to choose father in wealth within one heart pounding,
Worst and going to get Worster,
Evil persons of power upon the earth have cursed her,
Blood of innocents without repent,
Damaged the innocent goods with no goodness to uprise and have it spent,
When fall it meant to get up with thoughts of positive mannerism being from life in the way to shine the father in the life,

Then to fall is meant to never being honest to know the father in any mannerism from being of life in the way only the individual shine without truth in the life,

Dangers are ahead, keep calm have faith say prayers to be in bless,

Strangers are lead, sheep of the palm of father's faith from prayers from in bless,

One Night Stand

Dirty mind twinkles of cleanliness yet doing no harm in being foul can't be,

Adults agree to heat the time between them yet it's wrong in the law,

Not knowing this time spent can make the adults not be a danger to anyone, lord forgives, can't he?

The thrill to be of goodness is being in the dark experience weather did or around the dark actions to be at peace and not be of what you did or saw,

Being not of evilness with the time spent between two adults should be clean as a whistle, dear!

When there is no harm, no hurt being done from the heating action between two adults and making them sane, their souls are Bristol clear,

Yet no filth is allowed, so repent is the rule it clears all fouled,

Sin & Jail

L oud forgiveness leads to the truth of it,
    Sound forgiveness from the truth of sin,
I lost my way and led astray,
Yet been found in my day in the words of his may,
Knowing wrong in attention had the truth lit,
Glowing strong from detention in true sin,
Gave my belief power to father to not sin again, narrow path journey began,

Endless Thought

I feel Mathew's sorrow denying the King,
I hear no tomorrows' In Juda suicide from the King,
I fear the sexual legend of Mary known by the King,
I heal John belief in reality of the King,
As it I was posses to know I'm forgiven in all harden reality of life,
Came a great peace just to live in belief of Jesus in this reality of life,